Original title:
Where the Walls Stand Tall

Copyright © 2025 Creative Arts Management OÜ
All rights reserved.

Author: Samuel Kensington
ISBN HARDBACK: 978-1-80587-168-2
ISBN PAPERBACK: 978-1-80587-638-0

Shadows Among the Timbers

In the forest of beams, laughter will spring,
With squirrels in suits, doing their thing.
The owls hoot like DJs, spinning at night,
While trees hold their breath, for the comical sight.

Raccoons in pajamas, munching on snacks,
Debating the value of hiking with packs.
The sun peek-a-boos through the leaves with a grin,
As the shadows dance wildly, letting fun in.

Splinters of giggles bounce off the bark,
While frogs on the logs create quite the lark.
With whispers of echoes, the woodlands do prance,
In a merry old ballroom, they waltz and they dance.

In the Fortress of Solitude

In a castle of solitude, jesters do roam,
With clowns in the courtyard who won't leave you alone.
They juggle their worries and banish their fears,
While cats in capes dare the brave with their sneers.

The knights share their tales of embarrassing falls,
As banners of laughter hang high on the walls.
The goblets are filled with jokes, oh so sweet,
In this fortress of giggles, no one stays discreet.

In the dungeons, the echoes of chuckles resound,
As silliness flourishes, joy knows no bound.
For here in this castle, where laughter's the rule,
Everyone's welcome, especially the fool.

The Keeping of Secrets

Behind painted doors, whispers reside,
Each creak tells a tale that's hard to confide.
The walls lean in closer, ears made of stone,
Collecting the secrets they're urged to disown.

With chests full of treasures, both gold and absurd,
The gossiping fabrics spread rumors unheard.
The chandeliers chortle, they sparkle and sway,
As histories tumble like marbles in play.

With laughter's embrace, even shadows confide,
In this keeping of secrets, there's nowhere to hide.
So tiptoe on carpets and giggle with glee,
For the walls know your stories, as silly as we.

Embraced by Brick and Mortar

In a house full of bricks, the absurd takes its stand,
With each corner adorned by a slapstick hand.
The windows are laughing, the roof has a cheer,
As paint peels away, sharing secrets unclear.

Couches that bounce and giggle at night,
As lamps make bold jokes that give such delight.
The floors seem to rumble with snickers and grins,
For the house likes to party with all of its friends.

Though mortar may crack, and bricks may decay,
The humor lives on in a whimsical way.
So take off your shoes, let the silliness soar,
In this home full of laughter, there's always much more.

Rising Sentinels of Unyielding Fate

In a land where bricks go high,
They plot their schemes, oh my oh my.
Each brick a joke, a funny tale,
Guarding dreams 'till the sun turns pale.

How they stand, all stiff and proud,
Casting shadows on the crowd.
Yet whispered brawls between the stones,
Leave some grinning, others groans.

Watch them squabble 'bout the sky,
One claims it's too low to fly.
The other laughs and counters back,
'No flight tonight, just watch the crack!'

Yet through their gruff, their humor shines,
As laughter echoes 'cross the lines.
Even sentinels need to jest,
And give their weary frames some rest.

Reflections on the Edges of Sanctuary

At the edge, a mirror lies,
Reflecting humor, 'neath starlit skies.
A cheeky grin from walls so bold,
Sharing secrets, laughter told.

Each glance reveals a funny past,
Where jokes were tossed, shadows cast.
A wall once slipped, fell in a heap,
Dreaming of a job, just wanted to leap.

In the lines of bricks, a story spins,
Of dance-offs, and mock battles of wins.
The sanctuary giggles in delight,
As the night draws near, and walls take flight.

So raise a toast to guarding dreams,
In laughter's light, nothing's as it seems.
Where edges meet, the joy expands,
Creating fun in the toughest hands.

The Silence of Guarded Horizons

Amidst the quiet, walls stand strong,
But whispering giggles hum along.
They trade their tales, from brick to brick,
Making sure the past won't stick.

Unmoving guards with a spark of wit,
Shaking their heads at a joke well-fit.
A horizon jokes, 'I'm just a line,'
'Yet they call me the edge of divine!'

The silence sometimes breaks with cheer,
As walls brace up for a party near.
A dance of laughter, a tug of jest,
Who knew that walls could be so blessed?

In the quiet, the fun remains,
Making memories to shake off chains.
With their steadfast forms, they stand tall,
Yet it's their humor that conquers all.

Shadows Cast by Majestic Ramparts

Oh the shadows that giants throw,
Crafting silhouettes of tomfoolery, we know.
Majestic ramparts crack a smile,
As they guard the jesters all the while.

Each shadow plays a little trick,
Waltzing around, oh so slick.
A ghostly figure takes a bow,
While asking everyone, 'What's the row?'

From dusk till dawn, the fun abounds,
As the wall's laughter knows no bounds.
They wink as if to say with glee,
'Come join the fun, it's all for free!'

So let your worries drift away,
Amongst these giants, come what may.
In their shadows, laughter's found,
Exploring fun on hallowed ground.

The Embrace of Timeless Architecture

In a castle built for kings of yore,
The bathroom's lost, we search for more!
A staircase leads us round and round,
We laugh at echoes, what a sound!

The windows all are way too small,
Do we even fit? We might just fall!
Chasing shadows, dodging light,
This place could start a frightful flight!

With arches grand that stretch and bend,
I think I've found my new best friend!
A quirky wall outside the loo,
Oh, pardon me, is that a view?

Yet through the maze, we cheer and sing,
In this absurdity, joy we bring!
Though lost in heights and timeless grace,
I'd take this laugh over any place!

Chronicles of the Unyielding

Oh mighty brick, so proud and stout,
You guard our snacks, there's no doubt!
With tales of ages etched in stone,
I ponder if that's just a cone?

The towers lean, while we just cling,
As pigeons coo, oh how they sing!
We dance beneath the ancient beams,
And dodge the wall's intrigue-filled schemes!

With every crack, a story shared,
Of how I tripped; oh, I was spared!
This chorus of the wise old gate,
A perfect tune to celebrate!

So let this saga wane or grow,
Us silly fools, we steal the show!
In unyielding tales, we find our joy,
And laugh with walls that now annoy!

Beneath the Dawning Archway

A doorway wide, then narrow too,
I'm stuck! Is that a cue for you?
With playful arches, I make a dash,
And bump my head—what a crash!

As morning light seeps through each crack,
I swear I heard a ghost say 'smack'!
We prance through halls of dreamy frights,
Each shadowe's got peculiar bites!

These lofty tales of echoing cheer,
Where laughter dances, don't you fear!
With spoons for swords, we battle here,
In jest, in glee, shed every tear!

So let the dawn break bright and bold,
In this archway maze, let tales unfold!
With each step through halls of delight,
We're heroes in the morning light!

Serene in Steel and Stone

Steel beams wobble, oh what a sight,
Should I walk here? It feels so light!
In this fortress, where will I tread?
I might just slip, or worse, fall dead!

With stone so cold, yet smiles so warm,
We claim these halls, we start to swarm!
Buckets, ladders—tools of our trade,
We build a fort, our masquerade!

A fabric fortress, a peaceful scene,
Crafted here, where laughter's keen!
With every block and playful stare,
We redefine the art of air!

So raise your glass to this weird space,
Where architects forgot the grace!
In sturdy laughter, we are one,
In steel and stone, our race is fun!

Ruminations in the Hall of Shadows

In corners dark, a mouse plays chess,
Rats cheer him on, it's quite the mess.
The echoes laugh, they dance and twirl,
As shadows sip tea and start to swirl.

A startled bat drops a spoon with flair,
While a grumpy ghost combs its sparse hair.
The spider knits webs quite out of touch,
Saying, "Really, this fabric's too much!"

Amidst these walls, a riddle comes clear,
Why do the goblins keep drinking beer?

Sheltered by Ancient Limbs

Beneath the branches of a wisdom tree,
Squirrels tell jokes, laughing with glee.
Roots wiggle 'round, a playful ballet,
As mossy old limbs try to join the fray.

The wise old owl hoots, "Life's a great jest!"
While ants march on, thinking they're the best.
A raccoon pranks the porcupine crew,
With stolen snacks, then laughs, "Boo-hoohoo!"

The sun peeks in, it's a puzzling game,
All nature's actors, they play just the same.

The Tenderness of Toughness

A cactus pricks with a tender grin,
While a sturdy rock shakes off its kin.
"I'm rough around the edges, it's true!"
Says the pebble with charm in a jolly hue.

Amidst fierce storms, they sip sweet tea,
Cackling loudly, "Just let them be!"
A boulder sighs, "Why must we be tough?"
With a gentle smile, it says, "That's enough!"

They share silly tales of yesteryear,
Where softness shined bright, but no one could hear.

Lament of the Stone Traveler

A pebble rolls down a hill with a pout,
Screaming, "Not the ocean, I hate the route!"
He bumps off carelessly and mutters, "Great!
I'm destined for puddles or worse, a plate!"

He dreams of mountains, but faces defeat,
With every small splash, he's lost in the heat.
"Oh, to be dust, no path to alight,
Instead I'm just tossed in a wild flight!"

Each stone he meets just chuckles away,
"Life's quite a rush, in a twisty ballet!"

Tranquility in Stony Embrace

In a fortress made of bricks,
Lizard's tales and dusty tricks,
Echoes dance in sunlight's glow,
Packed with secrets we don't know.

Mice hold council, gossip spreads,
While spiders weave their loopy threads,
A throne of moss for ants so wise,
They plot their schemes and laugh at flies.

Gargoyles grin from their high perch,
While pigeons join the rooftop search,
Caught in clouds, the sun drips gold,
In stony calm, the tales unfold.

If walls could laugh, they'd bellow loud,
At human worries, all too proud,
So grab a snack, find a cozy nook,
Enjoy the show, life's a funny book.

Tales of the Bastion

Brick by brick, the stories grow,
Of knights who tripped with armor slow,
A jester's cap, a pie in flight,
The laughter echoes through the night.

Inside the stone, a cat parade,
Chasing shadows, no plans made,
They stumble over ancient lies,
In search of sunbeams and bird pies.

A ghost reviews his punchlines well,
His spectral humor cast a spell,
The cannonball's a comfy seat,
For laughter's echo, oh so sweet.

While guards stand watch with heavy sighs,
And dream of cakes and cream-filled pies,
In tales within this sturdy place,
There's always room for laughter's grace.

Beneath Archways of Memory

Under arches, whispers play,
Of stolen snacks and games at bay,
A broomstick horse, a knightly quest,
A pause for joy, no time for rest.

Laughter rides on echoes clear,
While dusty books hold tales sincere,
Of times when floors would start to creak,
And whispered secrets filled the week.

The mice plot feasts on crumbly tiles,
As giggles bounce in funny styles,
The old chandelier sways and sways,
As if it joins in childhood's plays.

With every noise, a laugh will bloom,
Reviving spirits in every room,
So come and linger, take a chance,
In memories' dance, let laughter prance.

The Keep of Obscured Truths

In a keep where truths get lost,
The pets discuss at a grand cost,
A taco here, a donut there,
Debating snacks beyond compare.

Books spin tales of time gone by,
Yet most of them just wonder why,
The king's hat somehow took a flight,
And turned the banquet into fright.

Guard dogs dream of chasing bees,
While cats conspire with playful ease,
The treasures here are jokes, not gold,
And so the legends start to mold.

As laughter rings through every hall,
With every stumble, every fall,
In a keep of whimsy, silly truths,
Are held in jest like playful sleuths.

Boundaries of the Heart's Stronghold

In a fortress made of giggles,
Constructed with a wobbly grin,
Adventures hide behind tall giggles,
Where silliness is kingpin.

A moat filled with bubbling dreams,
Swans that wear mismatched socks,
Guarding secrets with playful beams,
Time ticks with silly clocks.

Dreams bounce in every room,
As laughter bounces off the walls,
No room for any sense of gloom,
Only tickles and playful calls.

So come and dance in joy's parade,
Join the fun and leave your fuss,
In this heart's stronghold, we'll upgrade,
Our laughter, it shines bright and thus!

Shades of Stone in Twilight's Embrace

Under twilight's quirky glow,
Rocky shades with crazy cheer,
Each stone has a tale to tow,
With laughter that we hold dear.

Gargoyles grin with silly flair,
They crack jokes from their stone thrones,
In twilight's embrace, we share,
Chuckle with our silly phones.

The shadows throw a dance anew,
As giggles ripple through the night,
We find humor in the view,
Where every stone beams in delight.

In shades of dusk, we gleefully dwell,
With building blocks of joy to stack,
In twilight's embrace, so swell,
No need for courage—just laugh back!

Guardians of the Forgotten Grounds

In forgotten grounds where fools may tread,
Guarded by clowns with sillyy hats,
They play jokes on the sleepy dead,
On rocks that laugh at chatty rats.

The trees wear glasses, wise yet goofy,
Offering shade for a strike-up ball,
Squirrels debate who's more spoofy,
With chuckles echoing through it all.

Lost treasures of humor lie concealed,
Under a pile of giggling leaves,
In these grounds, laughter is revealed,
With playful tricks up our sleeves.

The guardians dance in moonlight's grace,
With each twinkle, a chuckle ensues,
In forgotten grounds, we find our place,
Where joy blooms and laughter brews!

Solid Emblems of Time's Passage

In solid walls, time takes a stand,
With pictures framed of foolish deeds,
Laughter echoes, nice and grand,
As we gather, the humor breeds.

The clocks tick-tock at silly pace,
Time's passage rendered in a jest,
With minutes that wear a funny face,
And hours that serve up endless zest.

Emblems tell our tales so bright,
Of all the pranks and mischief spun,
In shadows, we find sheer delight,
As past and present weave for fun.

So raise a toast to moments shared,
To walls that hold our laughter near,
In solid emblems, we are paired,
With joy that conquers every fear!

Chronicles of Grit and Fortitude

In a fortress made of cheese,
Where mice hold court with ease,
The bravest knight is quite a sight,
Fencing for crumbs in the moonlight.

They joust with forks and dance with glee,
With ketchup rivers; it's a sight to see,
A banquet for rats, a feast for all,
In a castle built of bouncy ball.

The Echoing Heartbeats of Sturdy Domains

Inside a tower full of fluff,
The guards are just too kind and rough,
They'd rather play a game of fetch,
With kittens draped across their sketch.

Echoes of laughter bounce off the walls,
As toddlers try to climb those halls,
The lord's a jester, what a show!
In acorn hats, they run to and fro.

Enclaves of Solitude and Serenity

In a quiet nook, a turtle's dreams,
Of lounging by bubbling streams,
His castle made of marshmallow soft,
Sipping tea, he's aloft!

A snail with a crown, oh what a pair,
They gossip as the daisies stare,
In shadows where the giggles bloom,
On silken sofas, they find their room.

Respite Found in Stone and Silence

In a cave that sings with a humor note,
Bats wear ties, you wouldn't gloat,
A rock band forms, it's quite the sight,
Their tunes are more like a playful fight.

Amidst the echoes, puns resound,
As echoes dance and spin around,
With each punchline, the walls do sway,
In a silent symphony of giggles play.

Sheltered by the Past

In a castle made of cheese,
The mice hold grand parades,
With knights in suits of bright Swiss,
They feast on fondue glades.

The walls are quite the chatter,
Echoing tales of yore,
Where once the king did flatter,
Now it's a mice galore.

A dungeon filled with laughter,
As jesters play their tricks,
The guards pursue the rafters,
In search of stolen brie sticks.

With every crumbling tower,
New jokes arise and bloom,
The ghosts all lose their power,
When punchlines fill the room.

Within the Stronghold's Heart

In a fortress built with giggles,
The ramparts dance and sway,
Where guards break into wiggles,
To keep the gloom at bay.

The moat's a swimming pool,
With rubber ducks afloat,
While knights act like a fool,
In their undies, they gloat.

The banners flap like kites,
As jesters spin and twirl,
Knights clash in silly fights,
For the last slice of pearl.

Amidst the ancient stone,
Laughter echoes so bright,
In this place, none alone,
Where humor takes its flight.

Boundaries Marked by Time

The walls of old are funny,
With cracks that grin and cheer,
Each stone a tale of honey,
Worn by the march of years.

The towers lean and giggle,
As wind whispers their quest,
And even moss will wiggle,
When it's put to the test.

Ghosts play hopscotch at night,
In the moon's silver beam,
Each step is pure delight,
As they dance and they beam.

Here, the past has no shyness,
It jests with every place,
In the stronghold's bright kindness,
There's always room for a race.

Secrets of the Ancient Keep

In the keep where secrets bide,
Cats hold court on high seats,
With feathers as their guide,
They plot with tiny feats.

The armor clinks with laughter,
As shadows play their tricks,
While knights sip on their nectar,
And plot their daring flicks.

A ghost spills potato salad,
Over the ancient map,
It's a feast of pure ballad,
For each hero caught in a hap.

With every door that creeks,
Lies a tale wrapped in jest,
In this fortress of mystique,
Humor truly knows best.

Evocations of Indomitable Spirits

In a castle made of cheese,
Knights ride on their knees.
Jousting with a loaf of bread,
Spectators laugh 'til they're red.

Lemons find a way to jest,
While cabbages feel blessed.
A dance with the parsnips bright,
In the glow of soft moonlight.

Crickets play a joyful tune,
As ants march round the moon.
Frogs host their grand parade,
In this land so unafraid.

So here's to spirits so spry,
Who find joy in the sky!
A toast to laughter so bold,
In tales of heroes retold.

A Lament for Hidden Spaces

In corners where dust bunnies dwell,
There's a laughter we all can smell.
Underneath the old, creaky stair,
A gnome wears nothing but flair.

Cracked tiles whisper old jokes,
As the mop dances with folks.
Beneath the fridge, a sock soldier,
Guarding crumbs, growing bolder.

Reality bends with a grin,
In nooks where oddities spin.
With each squeak of the floor,
We find treasures and lore.

Oh, hidden spaces so neat,
Where lost things and laughter meet.
We lament what we can't chase,
Yet cherish this quirky place.

Traditional Echoes in Modernity

A smartphone rings with a tune,
While grandpa's sock hops by the moon.
History serves tea with flair,
While memes scroll through the air.

Bagpipes play a techno beat,
As bagels dance to their own street.
Old tales with new-age twists,
As the cat creates wild lists.

Cousins in a virtual game,
Throwing eggs with endless aim.
In the kitchen, chaos glows,
While grandma hums as she throws.

Tradition does a pirouette,
In a program we won't forget.
Each echo finds its new home,
Where both old and new can roam.

The Crossroads within Indifference

At a fork in the road, a snail speaks,
"Choose wisely; don't wait for the weeks!"
Traffic cones wear party hats,
While pigeons dance, looking for chats.

The street signs throw a wild ball,
As passersby trip and fall.
Concrete jungle hums with glee,
While squirrels sip their herbal tea.

At the cusp of choices made,
A tumbleweed serenades.
Indifference waves back and forth,
While clowns march out to the north.

Should you wander, take your time,
At this strange crossroads, sublime.
For laughter reigns, as we assert,
In this whimsical, wobbly spurt.

In the Company of Giants

Beneath their shadows, I trip and fall,
These towering figures, they laugh at all.
With stone-cold faces, they play their part,
Yet in their company, I feel quite smart.

I asked a brick for some wisdom's grace,
It just replied with a silly face.
The windows giggle as breezes sigh,
While I, their jester, wonder why.

Each corner whispers a secret joke,
Of stubborn mortar and wily smoke.
The ceiling beams nod like they know best,
As I dance beneath their glaring jest.

In this odd place of grandeur and mirth,
I find my joy, my purpose, my worth.
No ordinary castle, this is my scene,
A kingdom where laughter reigns supreme.

Resilience in the Mortar's Grip

These bricks are grumpy, their faces set,
Stuck in place, they hold no regret.
Yet in their stoicism, I find my cheer,
As they grumble softly for all to hear.

A chip on the shoulder, a crack on the wall,
Every mishap becomes a humor-filled brawl.
The façade may crumble, but spirits won't break,
With laughter as glue, my heart won't shake.

Cracks tell stories of days gone by,
Of mischievous mice and a pizza pie.
The chimney shudders when I share a joke,
And the floorboards giggle, oh what a poke!

In this sturdy fortress, we hold our ground,
Among the echoes of giggles abound.
Mortar's embrace keeps us snug and tight,
In wild resilience, we find our delight.

Tales Told by Sturdy Edifices

The bricks gossip when no one's around,
Of one silly chimney that once fell down.
With every crack, a tale takes flight,
In buildings that chuckle through day and night.

"Remember the time when a squirrel raced by?
We nearly tipped over, oh my, oh my!"
The roof shakes with laughter, the beams sway in glee,
As elder walls share their history with me.

The paint peels slowly, revealing the fun,
Each flake a memory of pranks we've spun.
Dust motes dancing like a stand-up routine,
In this raucous laughter, my heart feels at ease.

So here I stand, with my pals made of stone,
Amidst the snickers, I've never felt alone.
Together we thrive in this whimsical space,
Where stories unfold with a grin on each face.

A Reverie among Stalwart Stones

In this daft dreamland of solid stone,
Even the statues look like they're prone,
To crack a smile, or at least a grin,
As I ponder the nonsense that lives within.

"Why so serious?" the columns all say,
Let's lighten our load, let's play, let's sway!
Though grounded and firm, they still find a way,
To laugh at the awkward who stumble and play.

A gnome on the ledge teases the moon,
While gardens of laughter bloom far too soon.
The steps creak a tune that's both funny and bright,
As we sway with the breeze in the shimmering light.

So let the stones stand, both sturdy and round,
With whispers of hilarity ringing around.
In this whimsical realm of granite and jest,
A reverie flourishes, we find ourselves blessed.

Myths from the Fortress

In a castle made of jelly beans,
Knights ride on toothy steeds.
They sip from goblets, bound by creams,
And dance on marshmallow meads.

Goblins play checkers with bears,
While wizards cook pies in the sky.
A dragon sings songs that declare,
He's allergic to cheese—you'll cry!

The moat's filled with silly-string goo,
As fairies make hats from the weeds.
Each legend we share is a brew,
Of giggles and sweets and good deeds.

So come, take a tour of this place,
Where laughter hangs thick in the air.
In the fortress, there's always a race,
To catch the last joke, if you dare.

Remembering the Shielded Past

Ancient tales of knights in tights,
Dancing in armor too tight to wear.
They fought with pillows in feathered fights,
While prancing like ducks in the square.

A squire once slipped on a banana peel,
And that led to a bouncy ball war.
With laughter that made the stones feel real,
The echoes of giggles galore!

The helmets are filled with jellyfish,
And shields serve a purpose astute.
If you ever should wish for a wish,
Just rub a helmet from a cute brute!

In this place where history's packed,
With tales of mishaps and pies,
Remember the knights and the laughter they lacked,
Bringing joy with every slip then rise.

Under the Watchful Eyes

Statues blink in the warm sunlight,
A knight nods, then sneezes with flair.
Their serious faces just aren't quite right,
When covered in cake—what a scare!

The turrets keep watch over picnic scenes,
As birds steal sandwiches with grace.
In this realm of odd-hued machines,
Even dragons know how to embrace!

A talking tree tells puns to the wind,
While squirrels hoard popcorn for the show.
With every giggle, the barriers thinned,
As laughter decides where to go.

So if you wander beneath arched skies,
And hear jests echoing near,
Know the place is alive with sly ties,
Woven with chuckles so dear.

Resonance of Hidden Corners

In nooks where the goblins play hide-and-seek,
Lay riddles that tickle the air.
A mouse with a mustache sings quite unique,
As turtles share secrets, so rare.

A cat wearing glasses reads books upside down,
While crickets debate with a hat.
No one really knows who wears the crown,
But the jesters just dance—what of that?

The shadows can giggle, the walls can laugh,
In corners where wisdom's risked.
Each echo a punchline, a comical half,
In the tapestry of tales that twist.

So wander in, where the odd things creep,
And let humor set you free.
For laughter, here, is a promise to keep,
In corners where mirth dares to be.

Fortresses Built of Hope and Dust

A castle made of empty dreams,
With turrets built from chocolate creams.
The moat's a pool of spilled surprise,
Where rubber ducks do roam and rise.

The knights are cats on guard all day,
Defending naps in their own way.
With armor made from tinfoil bright,
They chase the shadows, pounce, and bite.

The drawbridge sways on unsteady ropes,
While laughter bounces, full of hopes.
We feast on giggles, jokes, and cheer,
While dreams of glory fill the sphere.

So here we stand, with hearts aligned,
In crumbly towers, joy's enshrined.
With each quirk of fate, a tale to tell,
In fortresses built, we bask and dwell.

The Silent Language of Enduring Edifices.

Old bricks whisper secrets bold,
Of stories wrapped in dust and gold.
With every crack, a punchline gleams,
In echoes loud of childhood dreams.

The windows squint, they watch and play,
As squirrels dance in the light of day.
With rusty hinges, doors creak wide,
Inviting jesters in for a ride.

A roof of tiles, like hats askew,
Each shingle tells a joke or two.
And chimneys puff their smoke in cheer,
As laughter flows from far and near.

So stand we here, in strange delight,
With buildings chuckling in the night.
In silent humor, they reveal,
The joy of life, in bricks they seal.

Beneath the Weight of Stone

We sit beneath this bearded stone,
Where boulders giggle, never alone.
The ground beneath with roots so spry,
Tickles our feet as we walk by.

In shadows, goofy gnomes convene,
With mushroom hats, they plot unseen.
"A game of hide and seek," they cheer,
While echoes laugh, "Come find me here!"

The doors lead nowhere, or so they say,
A riddle here, a pun on display.
With arches that sway as if to tease,
They nod along with the rustling trees.

So let's chant rhymes beneath this weight,
Of hefty stones that contemplate.
In every crack, a sparkle's drawn,
With every jest, a new dawn spawned.

Echoes of Sturdy Sentinels

Tall sentinels with tales to tell,
Watch over lands where mischief dwells.
With creaky knees and eyes so wide,
They share their laughter, side by side.

With every gust, they shake and moan,
In friendly jest, they've overgrown.
The weathered stone, it cracks a grin,
As echoes bounce and tales begin.

They guard the secrets of silly pranks,
In shadows deep, they fill the ranks.
Gossip flows in breezy sighs,
As nature winks and slants her eyes.

So here we stand, tall and proud,
With sturdy sentinels, we're always loud.
In chuckles shared from walls around,
We find our joy in the absurd sound.

Through the Gaps of the Masonry

In the cracks, a squirrel peeks,
Searching for lost peanut treats.
Builders shook their heads and sighed,
Nature thinks outside, not inside.

Brick by brick, the tower stood,
While pigeons plotted mischief good.
A raindrop dances off the stone,
Lucy's umbrella flipped, she's flown.

Silent walls can hear the jokes,
From giggling mice and silly folks.
Concrete giants hold their pride,
While their shadows just can't hide.

At each gap, laughter fills the air,
A parrot sings without a care.
Oh, the secrets walls can share,
Who knew they had a sense of flair?

The Underbelly of Strong Structures

Beneath the beams, a party brews,
Dancing ants in zany hues.
The architect could never guess,
His designs could lead to such a mess.

Pillars tremble with glee and pride,
As mice in hats slip down the slide.
Caught beneath the weight of gloom,
Singing to lighten up the room.

The foundations giggle as they sway,
While drumming up a game to play.
Strength can't hide its playful side,
As every inch just wants to glide.

Beneath such might, the laughter rings,
As shadows dance with silly flings.
Who knew such heft could cause delight,
With silly smiles in every sight?

Possibilities in Round Edges

Curved and smooth, a secret plot,
To chase a dream that can't be caught.
Rollers take a wild, wild ride,
While squareheads stare, quite dignified.

A roundabout of merry cheer,
With laughter bouncing far and near.
Edges soft, like cotton candy,
While straight lines look a bit so dandy.

Twisting and turning, grooves entwined,
Circular jokes are truly designed.
Why did the wall refuse to play?
It claimed it wasn't 'round' that day!

The circular dance, oh what a sight,
As corners cringe in rigid fright.
Flexibility's where the fun can start,
In the realm of art, they play their part.

Traces of Light Through Grit

Sunlight peeks through the old cracks,
Creating shadows that dance, relax.
Where grit once held, now laughter beams,
Illuminating whimsical dreams.

Dust motes swirl in a waltz so bright,
Painted walls claim laughter's insight.
As grumpy bricks begin to chuckle,
A hidden door leads to a shuffle.

Each window frame finds a twist,
In the corners, sunlight kissed.
Grit may roughen what's within,
But joy will always find a spin.

So let the light jump in and play,
In a house that giggles all the way.
Each beam a story crafted from cheer,
As shadows whisper, "Come play here!"

Echoes of Enduring Shadows

In a hall of ghosts, I waltzed alone,
Echoing laughter, it made me groan.
Chasing my shadows, I slipped and tripped,
The walls all chuckled, I nearly flipped.

The chandeliers rattled, quite out of place,
While portraits grinned with a cheeky face.
I bowed to the echoes, they bowed right back,
In this dance of whims, we plotted a prank.

My sock once vanished, a comedy scene,
Caught under the couch, it made quite the mean.
The dust bunnies giggled, as I pulled and tugged,
In a fortress like this, it's laughter that's drugged.

So here I shall stay, in this jest of the years,
My walls, my partners, in joyful cheers.
Together we'll jest as the moonlight falls,
For nothing beats laughter when duty calls.

Embrace of Solitude's Fortress

In a cozy cell of my own design,
A fortress of solitude lined with wine.
I spoke to my dishes, they offered advice,
"Don't let the spoons mock you, that's just their vice."

Pillows my confidants, they never complain,
They hear all my secrets while I go insane.
My fridge is a hero, it knows all my needs,
Keeping the snacks safe, it never concedes.

From walls that confine, I still find delight,
A sock on the door, thinks it's taking flight.
My cat runs the garrison, a furry command,
With her stern little meows, she takes a bold stand.

The silence is golden, or purple, or green,
In my jokes with the curtains, I play the unseen.
So here in my kingdom, I wear the crown,
With puns on the walls, I will never frown.

Whispers Beneath the Sturdy Vault

Beneath the strong roof, my secrets reside,
Whispers of mischief, I can't always hide.
The beams cross and chatter, they tell silly tales,
Of chairs going rogue, and rebellious nails.

When windows start rattling, I giggle inside,
Imagining breezes as mischievous guides.
The doors creak with laughter, like they're in on a joke,
As I slip on my socks, they know I'll provoke.

With shadows that dance and the moon's silly grin,
I swear my strong walls are plotting to win.
Each corner a giggle, each crack an old friend,
In whispers of laughter, the fun will not end.

So here I shall dwell, in this lively embrace,
With walls that conspire, there's never dull space.
For a house full of joy is the best kind of fate,
And echoes of laughter are never too late.

The Resilience of Silent Sentinels

My walls are quite sturdy, but made of pure jest,
Guarding my humor, they're truly the best.
With cracks full of stories and paint chips that smile,
They've weathered my antics through every wild trial.

The corners are cozy, with dust motes that spin,
And light that comes in is a cheeky old grin.
As I stretch out my feet, the floorboards complain,
But they're loyal companions, sharing my pain.

The windows, they giggle, when breezes have fun,
And sunlight plays tricks on the walls, on the run.
I whisper my jokes to the sentinels standing,
Playing the fool, ever bold and demanding.

In this fort of fine walls, I cherish the chase,
Mischievous greeting in this solemn place.
With laughter my armor, I dance to the beat,
For the best kind of fortress is where giggles meet.

The Heartbeat of Solid Ground

In a house that hums with glee,
The floors brag of a lively spree.
Walls dance under laughter's sway,
As shadows play hide and seek all day.

In corners where the dust bunnies hide,
Lies a stash of socks that always slide.
Wobbly chairs hold secrets dear,
As the kettle screams, the end is near!

When the couch becomes a trampoline,
And pillows toss like an unseen machine.
Chasing echoes of giggles that roam,
Each room a kingdom, each nook a home.

So here's to the joy behind each frame,
The walls may stand tall, but they're never the same.
With every thud and joyous shout,
They hug our hearts and dance about!

Dreams Encased in Granite

In a fortress of dreams, I take my rest,
With granite walls that seem to jest.
They whisper tales of bacon fry,
While my alarm clock yawns and flutters by.

A bed that creaks with every toss,
As I ponder why the socks are lost.
Granite blocks don't seem to care,
They laugh along with my crazy hair!

Doors that squeak like a singing mouse,
Inviting in friends to my secret house.
Each step's a joke, a quirky pratfall,
Yet these sturdy stones, they cradle us all.

So here's to the laughter in each floor,
In a home where the drapes pretend to snore.
With dreams encased, both sweet and spry,
Granite giggles echo 'til morning's sky!

Echoed Longing in Quiet Chambers

In chambers where the echoes swell,
A cat's soft purr, a secret spell.
Whispers float like feathers in flight,
Making even the shadows giggle at night.

The fridge hums tunes of creamy delight,
Yet it outshines me in the kitchen's light.
A cupboard holds a treasure trove,
Of snacks to nibble and stories to rove.

Walls may listen to dreams I weave,
Yet the creaks at night, they don't believe.
Each room a canvas of laughter and cheer,
While I stumble on crumbs, oh look, there's a beer!

So here's to the echoes that surround,
In quiet chambers, joy is found.
With every chuckle, every sigh,
The walls join in, oh my, oh my!

The Lords of the Threshold

In the land of doorways, we reign supreme,
With knobs that jiggle and often scheme.
We usher in laughter, we're never shy,
As we trip over shoes and let out a sigh.

Welcome mats know all the tales,
Of muddy boots and epic fails.
They gossip about socks that don't match,
And sneaky cats that thought it a catch!

The lords preside with a wobbly stance,
As we dance around in a jolly prance.
Each entrance a stage, each leaky frame,
Turns every visit into a silly game.

So here's to the thresholds, old and wise,
They've seen it all with a twinkle in their eyes.
With every footstep and every knock,
They cheer us on like the comical clock!

Beneath the Sentinel's Gaze

In the city where pigeons plot,
A general takes lessons from a robot.
Cats on rooftops hold meetings at noon,
While squirrels practice their best cartoon.

Grass grows wild on tired old bricks,
Neighbors share tales of their wild cat tricks.
The statue looks on, with a bemused stare,
As children play tag, forgetting their care.

Heat waves shimmer like disco lights,
While cats conduct secret morning rites.
The squirrels proclaim a snack parade,
In this place, no worry, all problems fade.

So here we gather, in laughter and cheer,
Under the gaze of that sentinel here.
Let's dance through the chaos of life just as planned,
With antics that tickle—oh, isn't it grand?

The Silent Watchers of the Night

Bats wear capes made of midnight cloth,
While owls argue over who's got the sloth.
Stars gossip lightly on their shining stage,
The moon giggles softly, feeling quite sage.

Creepy shadows with jokes to share,
Phantom friends float on the cool night air.
Fireflies twinkle in their glow-up show,
While raccoons search for the best taco flow.

Under the streetlight, a dance party starts,
With crickets playing their tiny little parts.
Whispers and chuckles in dark corners sprawl,
As the night keeps handing out laughter to all.

So let's toast to the night with our fanciful dreams,
To mischief and joy and the odd silly schemes.
For in this darkness, we find a delight,
Among silent watchers, we laugh through the night.

Dreams Woven with Iron and Stone

Iron giants in a huddle discuss,
While cobblestone holds secrets in a fuss.
The fountain gurgles a playful tune,
As pigeons debate, should they swoop or moon?

With every crack in the pavement so grand,
A tale unfolds, led by a wise rubber band.
The towers yawn, stretching tall and wide,
While echoes of laughter fill every stride.

A cupcake on a pedestal waits to inspire,
As dreams mix with laughter, fueled by desire.
The shadows join in, dancing with flair,
Twirling in circles like they haven't a care.

Among bricks and mortar, we spin our own yarns,
With a hint of mischief, a dash of charms.
So let's weave together, in giggles we trust,
In this world bound by whimsy, love, and some rust.

In the Shadow of the Apex

High on the roof, a chicken contemplates,
While a mouse in a top hat ponders life fates.
Beneath the apex, all creatures unite,
In a world that finds humor in taking to flight.

The wind whispers secrets to the old oaks,
As turtles crack jokes, sharing their pokes.
With squirrels in tuxedos and feathery hats,
They throw fancy parties, inciting more spats.

Graffiti whispers stories so bold,
While pigeons tell tales of journeys untold.
Colors of laughter paint the city bright,
As shadows bounce back with a wink of delight.

So come share a laugh in this playful parade,
Where whimsy and fun are beautifully displayed.
In the shadowed heights, we'll create our own quest,
In a jumble of joys, may we ever be blessed!

The Weight of Solitude's Embrace

In a room that's big and bare,
A cat plays solitaire with air.
A sock that vanished, no one knows,
It hides with the dust and eerie doze.

The fridge hums jokes from days gone by,
A lonely fish sticks to the fry.
Lampshades whisper tales of yore,
While cobwebs dance and settle the score.

Mirror reflects a curious chap,
Who talks to the walls, then takes a nap.
A time traveler's scheme gone askew,
In heels, no less, that look like a shoe.

So here's to the space that laughs and lingers,
Filling the silence with jokes of fingers.
Embrace the echo, let giggles roll,
Amidst solitude's weight, discover your soul.

Resilient Dreams Behind Sturdy Barriers

Behind big doors and sturdy gates,
A squirrel builds dreams on broken plates.
Nuts and bolts in a dance so grand,
Imagine a world where they take a stand.

The paint is peeling, oh what a sight,
But the weeds grow taller, oh, what a fight!
They giggle and wiggle, take on their own,
Making a kingdom, all overgrown.

A garden gnome dreams of a pie,
That flies like a bird and sings in the sky.
He twirls with the daisies, chases the bees,
And wishes for ketchup—oh, how it frees!

So let the walls hum a loyal tune,
As raccoons dine fine, beneath the moon.
In these sturdy spaces where laughter remains,
There's a riot of dreams, like balloons on trains.

The Quiet Majesty of Enduring Structures

A tower stands, regal and wise,
With pigeons that mock the clouds in the skies.
They boast of travel, yet never roam,
To coo a sweet song, and call it home.

The cracks in the plaster, a puzzle to solve,
While ants get lost in a mini-resolve.
Every peep you hear is a hall of fame,
Where echoes revel and chatter the same.

Painting in layers the colors of past,
Where gardens grow wild, but pigeons fly fast.
Here in retreat, the humor unfolds,
As bricks relay secrets that nobody told.

Majestic the stillness, with comical quirks,
As laughter joins in with the creaks and the jerks.
In sturdy embrace, it's clear to see,
Life weaves its fabric in jocular glee.

Traces of Life Amidst Stalwart Walls

In the shadow of walls that gleam and shine,
A raccoon holds court with a glass of wine.
He tells tales of treasures from bins nearby,
While passersby wonder, with a curious eye.

The stairs creak a tune, a wobbly dance,
As dust bunnies plan a daring romance.
They laugh as they leap from shelf to shelf,
Pretending they're dating—oh, look at themselves!

Chairs giggle in corners, they've earned their keep,
Resting their legs while the curtains peek.
In these cherished spots, memories collide,
With coffee stains and sweet pride worldwide.

Yet every crack hides a jaunty smile,
Inviting us to stay for a while.
So raise a toast to the laughter it brings,
As life sprinkles joy on the old sturdy things.

Eternal Watchers of the Lonely Streets

The bricks all gossip, so they say,
About the things that come and play.
A cat in a hat, a man with a shoe,
They laugh at the chaos, it's all true!

With every tap of a passing shoe,
Those walls lean in to hear the view.
Whispers of secrets, silly and spry,
A pair of ducks just taking a fly.

They've seen the dances of blooms in spring,
And all the joy that laughter can bring.
Yet, when it's quiet, oh how they mope,
Staring out, clutching the dreams of hope.

But wait! A squirrel with a peanut stash,
Dashes by like a comedic flash.
"Hey walls, did you see that uptight hog?"
Their laughter echoes, a fun dialogue!

Secrets Kept Beneath Weathered Skies

Beneath the clouds that seem to poke,
The walls sigh gently, then they joke.
"Did you spot that bird, so proud and rare?
The one who thinks she's a millionaire?"

The breeze carries giggles, softly drawn,
As shadows stretch over the sleepy lawn.
Walls chuckle low, their spirits high,
At thoughts of a tortoise lost in July.

Raindrops tickle, like playful teens,
Dancing about in quirky routines.
With each splash, they share a cheer,
Making life fun, year after year.

So when the sun makes walls grow bold,
They share their tales, both new and old.
"Tomorrow's storm?" one wall tries to guess,
"Will it bring puddles or just a mess?"

Stalwart Sentinels of Forgotten Paths

In the corners where shadows play,
The walls giggle in old-fashioned way.
"Remember that tripled-up old guy?
He tipped his hat, but forgot to fly!"

Guarding paths both lost and found,
They chuckle at footsteps all around.
A child who slips on a muddy shoe,
Walls ponder what more mischief he'll do.

They witness the runners, quick and spry,
And giggle at as they stumble by.
"Hey walls, did you catch that wild fall?"
"Just another day in fun, after all!"

In silence, they keep their laughter grand,
Echoing joy through all the land.
So if you wander where memories call,
Listen closely to the walls—that's all!

Emblems of Strength in the Heart of Stillness

In stillness, they wear a grin so wide,
Those steadfast walls, full of pride.
"Why stand so strong," a butterfly quips,
"When the world's full of hilarious slips?"

They recall the antics of kids at play,
Jumping over puddles in a joyous ballet.
"Did the ice cream cone really fall?"
"Oh yes, right on his friend's back, that's all."

Observing the sun-baked cracks of age,
They laugh at each joke, each new page.
With every creak, a tale they tell,
Of laughter shared, and all is well.

So hold your breath on a breezy eve,
For walls, they're the best at what they weave.
Underneath the weight of endless time,
They dance in memories, a silly rhyme.

The Watchtower's Soliloquy

Up high I watch the silly dogs chase,
They think they run, but they just take space.
With every bark, I giggle and tease,
These furry jesters, oh, they're such a breeze.

The villagers shout, 'What do you see?'
A soaring pigeon, or perhaps a bee?
But perched on my tower, my thoughts run wild,
I plot pranks on passers-by, oh, how they smiled!

With comical tales of ghosts in the night,
I imagine a world where they give a fright.
A broomstick instead, would bring such a laugh,
At the break of dawn, I'll prepare my craft.

From my tall perch, I wave to the crow,
"Do you know my secrets? Come, let's put on a show!"
With a flip of the wing, he caws out loud,
Echoing laughter, I'm the king of the crowd!

In the Cellar of Echoes

Deep in the cellar, I find all the wine,
Each bottle with stories and a quirky line.
I hear clinking laughter in the dark below,
An echoing party, it's quite the show!

Dust bunnies mingle, they're dancing with glee,
Spinning around on a mud pie spree.
The jars and the cans join in with a chime,
Together they chortle—they've got such good rhyme!

I pour out some vintage, it starts telling tales,
Of clumsy knights and their ambitious fails.
With every sip, the laughter grows loud,
As the echoes of jokes encompass the crowd!

So while the moon frowns on their rusted old plight,
The cellar keeps secrets and celebrates light.
In the depths of the cobwebs, I'll be the king,
With echoes of jest, let the merriment ring!

The Fortress of Forgotten Whispers

In the fortress of whispers, secrets unwind,
An ant sneezed loudly—oh, isn't he blind?
The stones are all giggling, they render a jest,
At the poor little bug who just wanted to rest.

Around every corner, the ghosts play a game,
Of peekaboo antics—such an embarrassing fame!
They tickle the shadows with a silvery thread,
While the stones roll their eyes, shaking their head.

A knight walks in, tripping over his shoe,
He's searching for glory, but finds a ballyhoo.
"Who's there?" he yells, while the spirits all cackle,
But the fortress just quivers and offers him a tackle.

With echoes of laughter, the walls come alive,
Telling tales of mishaps, where no one can thrive.
In this quirky stronghold, humor never fails,
As we bop through the tales, through whispers and gales!

Unyielding Presence of the Past

Upon the old stairs, I trip with a flair,
"Oh, look at me!" I shout to the air.
The past holds its laughter, it echoes my fall,
Brick by aged brick, it just loves to sprawl.

The relics are chuckling, they've seen better days,
A dusty old clock gives me teasing displays.
"Time's not on your side," it chimes with a wink,
I grin back at it, with a pause and a blink.

The portraits are smug, in their gilded frames,
With expressions aflutter, they play silly games.
I mimic their frowns, but it's hard not to grin,
These guardians of history, let the laughter begin!

In corners of memory, I dance with delight,
To the tune of forgotten, in the soft pale light.
So here I'll abide, amidst chuckles and sighs,
With the past as my comic—what a charming surprise!

Archive of the Unspoken

In a room filled with echoing cheer,
Books whisper secrets, oh so near.
Dust bunnies dance in the light,
While a cat dreams away the night.

Old chairs creak with tales to share,
As mice plot mischief without a care.
Every glance at a dusty tome,
Makes you wonder if they call it home.

A ghost in the corner plays a tune,
With a quill that buzzes like a bumble moon.
They argue about who's the wisest sage,
While a spider spins webs on a yellowed page.

Banners hang with colorful flair,
Yet no one cares to fix the tear.
Every hour's a comedic scene,
As paper ghosts tease, "What does that mean?"

Solace in the Strength of Stone

Rocks wear smiles, or so they claim,
As they play hide-and-seek in the game.
A statue sneezes, the pigeons fly,
And giggles echo as the squirrels sigh.

Moss gathers gossip from every nook,
While crickets rehearse a Broadway book.
Boulders chuckle with canine glee,
Saying, "We're tougher than any tree!"

Puddles form laughter from rainy days,
With reflections that twist in silly ways.
Every raindrop, a ticklish thrill,
As stones chuckle, "We don't need a hill!"

In laughter's embrace, the walls hold tight,
Guardians of giggles through day and night.
Even in silence, jokes are stored,
Within these stones, so much adored.

The Echoing Passage

In the tunnel, echoes play,
With voices that have gone astray.
"Watch your step!" they gleefully shout,
As shadows dance and twirl about.

Raccoons debate the best pathways,
As echoes laugh at their silly ways.
"Let's take a left!" one boldly calls,
Only to end up in a game of balls.

Footsteps tap like a lively band,
The walls are clapping, oh so grand!
With every turn, a joke unfolds,
In the dim light, their laughter molds.

Through every inch that joy provides,
Even the darkness stands and hides.
This passage whispers, without a care,
"Don't take life too seriously, beware!"

Stories Bound by Cedar and Stone

In a cabin where secrets like to stew,
The cedar smells of tales askew.
Gnarled branches play a twangy tune,
While squirrels argue if it's too soon.

Windows rattle with laughter's grace,
As the chips on the table keep pace.
Logs piled high begin to chat,
"Ever thought a potato could wear a hat?"

Old wainscoting holds tales like glue,
Whispers of mischief from days anew.
In every knot, a joke is trapped,
Awaiting a story so brightly wrapped.

The laughter lingers, the fire crackles,
As wildlife prances where the humor tackles.
In this nook of frank and free,
Walls chuckle in perfect harmony.

Whispers Behind Stalwart Gates

In the shadows, secrets roam,
Like squirrels with acorns, they claim the dome.
A giggle here, a laugh over there,
Those sturdy gates make quite the pair.

With every creak, a chuckle sounds,
As light-footed mice conspire in bounds.
The walls, they listen with a grin,
As whispers swirl, a raucous din.

A parrot jokes, perched high above,
And the stone gargoyle looks on with love.
With every jest, the fortress beams,
Echoing softly our silly dreams.

So come on in, leave worries behind,
In these strong walls, pure fun you'll find.
For even the bricks have got a joke,
In the laughter of life, let's all provoke.

Guardians of the Silent Halls

Old portraits stare with painted smiles,
While shadows sneak through dusty aisles.
A guardian cat, with eyes so sly,
Winks at the mice who scurry by.

Each echo bounces, plays a trick,
As chandeliers sway, the pendulum's tick.
The floors' old creaks sound just like laughs,
Hiding away from the echoing gaffes.

The suits of armor rattle with glee,
Like jesters in a court, catapulted free.
The silent halls burst into song,
With every footstep, you can't go wrong!

So tiptoe lightly, let laughter rise,
Among the guardians with twinkling eyes.
In the halls where whispers chill,
A ticklish spirit is waiting still.

Strength in Every Corner

In the corners, mysteries dance,
Like those old socks that chance a glance.
Each cranny laughs, a merry face,
Echoing jokes through this sturdy place.

Chairs that squeak with tales of woe,
Adventurous rugs say, 'Don't be slow!'
Lamps nod softly, guiding the way,
Creaking with mirth as night turns to day.

Windows chatter with breezy flair,
While walls hoot tales from way up there.
A tale of a cat who chased his tail,
In every corner, giggles prevail!

So clap your hands and stomp your feet,
Join the walls in this merry beat.
For strength is not just in the stone,
But in the laughter that turns to home.

The Echo Chamber of Dreams

In a chamber where echoes freely play,
Dreams bounce back in a quirky way.
'Pillow fights' turn into roars and cheers,
As laughter glides through the years.

The curtains whisper, the curtains sigh,
Bouncing sounds of a jumpy pie.
Footsteps rattle in merry delight,
Chasing echoes into the night.

Mirrors giggle at every turn,
Reflecting mischief, the walls do yearn.
As dreams pirouette, they twirl around,
In this echo, pure joy is found.

So let your spirit wander, my friend,
In the chamber where giggles ascend.
For each echo we send into the night,
Returns with laughter, dark into light.

Towers of Unspoken Dreams

In a town where folks are shy,
The gossip flies like birds on high.
Walls with secrets, laughter stowed,
Chasing tales down the old road.

Pigeons coo and roll their eyes,
As humans spin their wildest lies.
A fortress built of giggles and grins,
Catapulting stories where mischief begins.

They say the bricks are thick with cheer,
While the world outside feels far and near.
In towers high, dreams take flight,
While neighbors peek from left and right.

So raise a toast to concrete fanciful,
For every joke turns out quite practical.
Here we stand, no need for charm,
Our fortress of fun, keeps us warm!

The Stillness of Fortified Echoes

Echoes bounce off sturdy walls,
Where whispers mingle, and laughter calls.
In the midst of silence reigns,
A dance of shadows, silly gains.

Squirrels scamper with acorn delight,
As pigeons strut, taking flight.
A fortress filled with secrets shared,
Behind each wall, a jest is aired.

The stillness crackles with hidden glee,
As laughter peeks from around a tree.
What's that noise? Oh, it's just the breeze,
Swirling gossip with such ease.

Behind these walls, we'll find our quirks,
Bouncing off like playful sparks.
With every grin, our spirits swell,
In this snug space, all's well.

Veils of Strength in Quiet Reflections

Silent veils as strong as steel,
Hide the secrets folks conceal.
In stillness, jokes lay dormant, too,
Waiting for the perfect cue.

Reflections in the window panes,
Tell of laughter that never wanes.
A witticism stuck in flight,
Just like the cat who forgot the night.

Strength in silence, oh so grand,
With every giggle tightly planned.
Behind each veil, a smirk appears,
The walls stand tall, absorbing cheers.

With every glance, the humor grows,
In the echoes of snorts and throes.
We'll keep our mirth, our hearts entwined,
In the quiet corners, laughter's designed.

Monoliths of Memory's Embrace

Monoliths stand with a knowing grin,
Holding tales of where we've been.
Memories wrapped in laughs we find,
Echoing softly, joy redefined.

The walls know all our quirks and slips,
Decades of joy and strange flicked lips.
A stubborn cat with a penchant for fun,
Chasing shadows, never done.

With each stumble, we roar and shout,
As laughter transforms every doubt.
These mighty towers are strong yet spry,
In their embrace, our spirits fly.

So dance among the towering stones,
Crafting jests in cushioned tones.
For every brick, a punchline laid,
In memory's arms, we play unafraid.

Tales from the Crumbling Edges

Once a wall had dreams to soar,
But it tripped and fell, oh what a chore!
It tried to dance but lost its form,
Now it leans like a friend in a storm.

The bricks would gossip, oh what a sight,
About the squirrel who danced all night.
With cracks for laughter, they shared their tales,
Of roof rats that ran like they had big sales.

A window once winked at a tree,
"Come on, let's make mischief, just you and me!"
But the tree just chuckled and shook its leaves,
"You can't go outside; it's not in your dreams!"

So here they stand, crumbling and old,
With funny stories that never get told.
They create a world of silly delight,
Amid crumbling edges, there's always a bite.

The Solace of Stone

In the village of bricks, a stone sat tight,
Said, "I'm the king of this crumbling sight!"
But a pigeon flew in, with feathers so grand,
Told the stone, "Sit down, you don't make a stand!"

The stone replied, "Look at my face!
I may be slow, but I own this place!"
But the pigeon just cooed, doing a twirl,
"In this dance-off, you're a stone in a whirl!"

Moss tickled the edges, a green joke to spread,
As the stone grumbled loud, it was barely red.
"Why can't I dance? Why can't I groove?
Instead, I just stand and watch you move!"

They filled the square with whimsical lights,
Where stones became jesters, and pigeons took flights.
In a kingdom of laughter, they claimed their throne,
With funny tales, they'll never be alone!

Frosted Memories in Sturdy Reinforcements

In winter's chill, a wall stood proud,
With frost like diamonds, it looked real loud.
A snowman chuckled, draped in a scarf,
"You think you're so tough? Let's see you laugh!"

The wall just shivered, couldn't express,
With icicles hanging like frozen stress.
But a rabbit hopped by with a grin so wide,
"Join me for cocoa, let's laugh through the ride!"

They built up a frost castle, oh what a sight,
The wall said, "I'm strong! I can't take flight."
But the rabbit just giggled, making it clear,
"Even sturdy things can melt with good cheer!"

So they shared hot cocoa and stories to tell,
Two friends in the cold, under snowflakes that fell.
Amid heavy frost, they melted the fail,
In chilly friendship, they crafted a tale.

Between the Columns of Yesterday

Two columns stood proud, once guardians tall,
Now they reminisce about the grand ball.
"Do you remember the dance? Oh what a sight!"
"A tumble and roll, I slipped out of fright!"

They chuckled and nudged, their mortar so frail,
"Why did the chicken cross? To hear our tale!"
With each passing pigeon, they scratched their stone heads,
"It's better than crumbles, our tales can spread!"

A stray cat strolled in with a saunter so sweet,
"Hey columns, you're stiff! Get up on your feet!"
"You're a cat! You can climb, while we hold the shore!"
But she just rolled over, purring for more.

As birds danced around, making all of their calls,
The columns stood proud, embracing their falls.
In laughter and tales, they found their great spot,
The past echoed gently, all in a funny plot.

In the Tender Clutch of Stability

In a fortress made of cheese,
We dance with mice as they tease.
A ladder in the pantry high,
Leads to cookies we can't deny.

Potato chips like armor cling,
As we pretend to be a king.
With squirrels plotting from above,
We laugh and build our dreams of love.

Debates with pigeons in the park,
Who knew they'd outshine Noah's ark?
In cozy corners, wild dreams form,
Our laughter keeping us both warm.

But rock and roll of life's parade,
In clown shoes, we'll forever wade.
With structures made of ice cream treats,
Stability is where chaos meets.

Resilience Framed by the Sky

Under the umbrella of a cake,
We brave the storms that make us quake.
With cupcakes, donuts at our sides,
We surf the clouds on wild slides.

Sunshine drones with melodies blare,
As we twirl like we haven't a care.
Each sprinkle brightens up the day,
In our fortress, we choose to play.

The moon's a giant disco ball,
Inviting us to dance and sprawl.
A cacophony of silly sounds,
In laughter, joy is where we're found.

So come, let's hop on jelly beans,
We'll bounce through life in silly scenes.
With resilience dressed in party hats,
Together we'll dodge life's silly spats.

The Whirl of Life Against Resistance

Round and round, the wheels will spin,
With outfits made of socks and skin.
A noodle fight in the breeze,
Our laughter flows, it's sure to please.

Through every twist, our joy will leap,
In messy kitchens, secrets keep.
With flour clouds and eggy splats,
We let the cake mix take us flat.

Each leap robust, like jelly's jig,
We misfit neatly, oh how big!
In shoes too tight, we waddle on,
Like penguins with an inner song.

But when the world grows faint and dull,
We'll bring the circus with our pull.
For through the whirl, let's find our glee,
In every twist, we'll just be free.

Gatherings Beneath the Ancient Beams

Beneath the beams of ancient trees,
We giggle quietly in the breeze.
With hats that wobble and shoes that squeak,
Our voices rise, it's fun we seek.

The squirrels gossip, oh so loud,
As we perform before the crowd.
With tales of heroes, dogs, and cats,
In pajama pants, we strike poses, flats.

A feast of puddings lays in wait,
In muddy boots, we celebrate.
With legends made of silly dreams,
We toast to life with giggles and screams.

So, let's shout secrets to the stars,
And make up words from near and far.
Together under leafy beams,
We'll chase our joy beyond our dreams.

www.ingramcontent.com/pod-product-compliance
Lightning Source LLC
Chambersburg PA
CBHW070305120526
44590CB00017B/2573